Splish Splash Splosh!

by Mick Manning
and
Brita Granström

W

FRANKLIN WATTS
LONDON•SYDNEY

sheen montessori nursery

Good Luck
at
Big School ☺

Splish, Splash, Splosh!

Waves hit the beach.
They come roaring in only to trickle away.
Where do they come from and where do they go?

Waves are caused by the winds and tides.

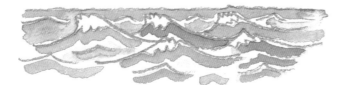

2

Splish, Splash, Splosh!

Waves dance near the shore –
slop under boats and ships,
slap against harbours and jetties.

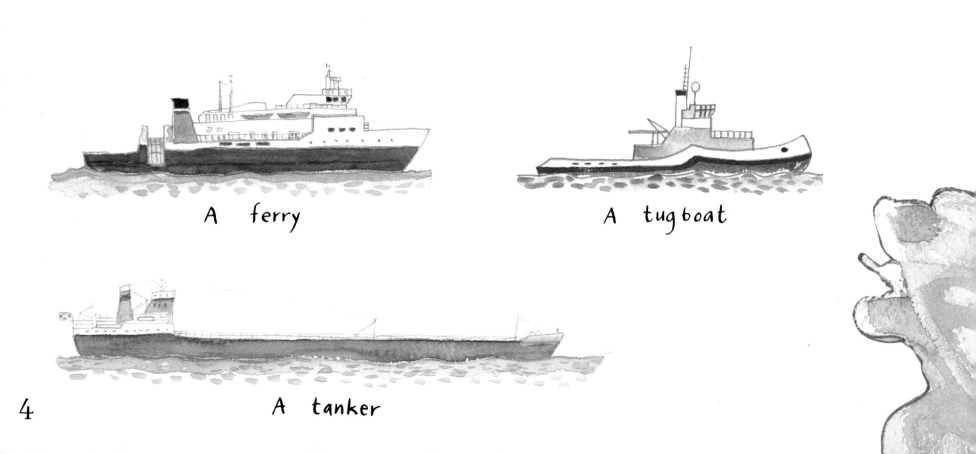

A ferry

A tugboat

A tanker

5

Splish, Splash, Splosh!

Far out to sea where the water is deep, seawater washes over dolphins' backs and between sharks' teeth...slips through shipwrecks and coral reefs.

Parts of the sea are so deep huge mountain ranges can lie under the surface.

Giant octopuses and many other creatures live deep under the sea.

Splish, Splash, Splosh!

On hot days, the sun sucks tiny droplets of water into the sky. Clouds form and drift above the crashing waves. Sea breezes blow them far away – high in the sky they sail inland like ships.

Clouds are formed from tiny droplets of water.

Sometimes frogs and even small fish can be sucked up into the clouds and fall with the rain somewhere else!

Splish, Splash, Splosh!

Clouds heavy with water gather over the land and swirl into a storm. Raindrops burst from the clouds and fall to earth.

Some countries have rainstorms called monsoons. Monsoons can destroy buildings and flood towns.

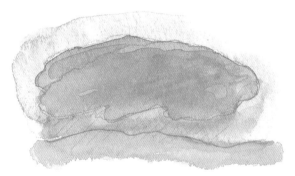

Different sorts of clouds...

fine day clouds

thunder clouds

grey day clouds

Splish, Splash, Splosh!

Rainwater trickles down the hillsides...
makes puddles...flows wild and muddy
into streams.

Every living thing needs water to survive!

Splish, Splash, Splosh!

Streams rush headlong into a crazy waterfall,
that crashes into a river that swells and swells...
and fills up a dam.

A rainbow is made when the sun shines through tiny drops of water in the air.

The colours of a rainbow are red, orange, yellow, green, blue, indigo and violet.

Splish, Splash, Splosh!

In the dam, muddy water clears.
Fish live in the dam, they swim around a pipe
that takes the water down to filters and
cleaning tanks.

Water must be cleaned before we can drink it ...

Dams, reservoirs and underground wells are places where we store water.

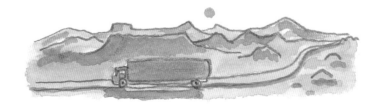

In times of drought when there is not much rain, water has to be delivered by tanker.

Splish, Splash, Splosh!

Water travels for miles – under fields, hills,
roads and motorways to an underground reservoir.
Then it joins the mains water supply to towns,
villages, factories, hotels, offices and houses...
to your house!

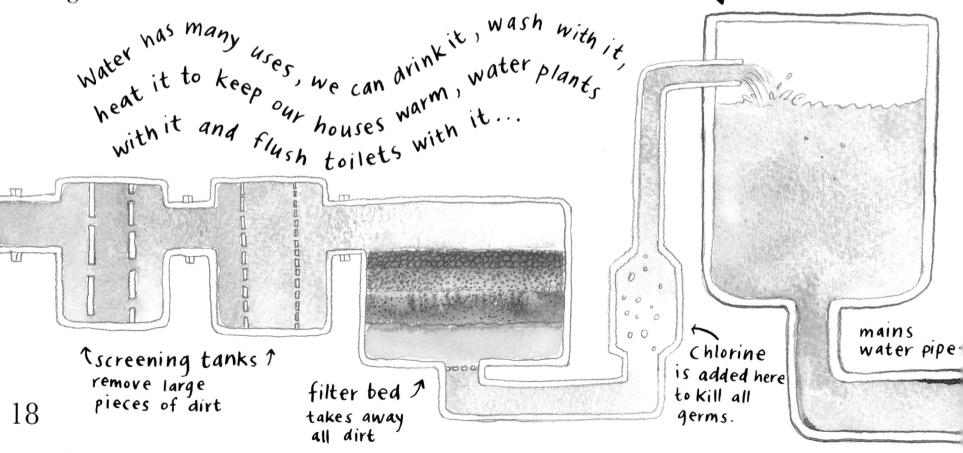

Water has many uses, we can drink it, wash with it, heat it to keep our houses warm, water plants with it and flush toilets with it...

underground reservoir-
stores the water

↑screening tanks ↑
remove large
pieces of dirt

filter bed ↗
takes away
all dirt

Chlorine
is added here
to kill all
germs.

mains
water pipe

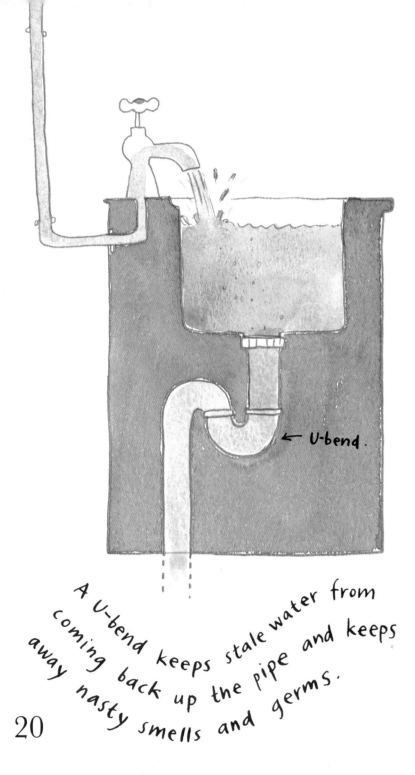

← U-bend.

A U-bend keeps stale water from coming back up the pipe and keeps away nasty smells and germs.

Splish, Splash, Splosh!

You have a wash.
Clean water splutters out of the taps... out of the shower. Then soapy water escapes down the plughole, down a plastic pipe and down the drain.

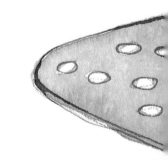

Rats are very common down sewers all over the world. They spread diseases so most cities employ 'ratcatchers'.

Splish, Splash, Splosh!

Under the street, bathwater mixes with other waste water – sink water and toilet water.

Sometimes unwanted pets — tropical fish and even alligators have been found in sewers. They'd been flushed down the toilet!

It runs along sewer tunnels as big as subways and becomes thick and sludgy.

Splish, Splash, Splosh!

Waste water flows out into the sewage farm.
It pushes through sieves, dribbles through screens,
squeezes through filters and bubbles through blowers.
Water leaves sludge behind and is piped out.
It trickles and gushes back to the...

Water is piped through special tanks to clean it.

Sea!

Splish, Splash, Splosh!

a water map

We have to be very careful and keep water clean – We all need it to stay alive!

the Sun

clouds

the Sea

fores[t]

sewage farm

beach

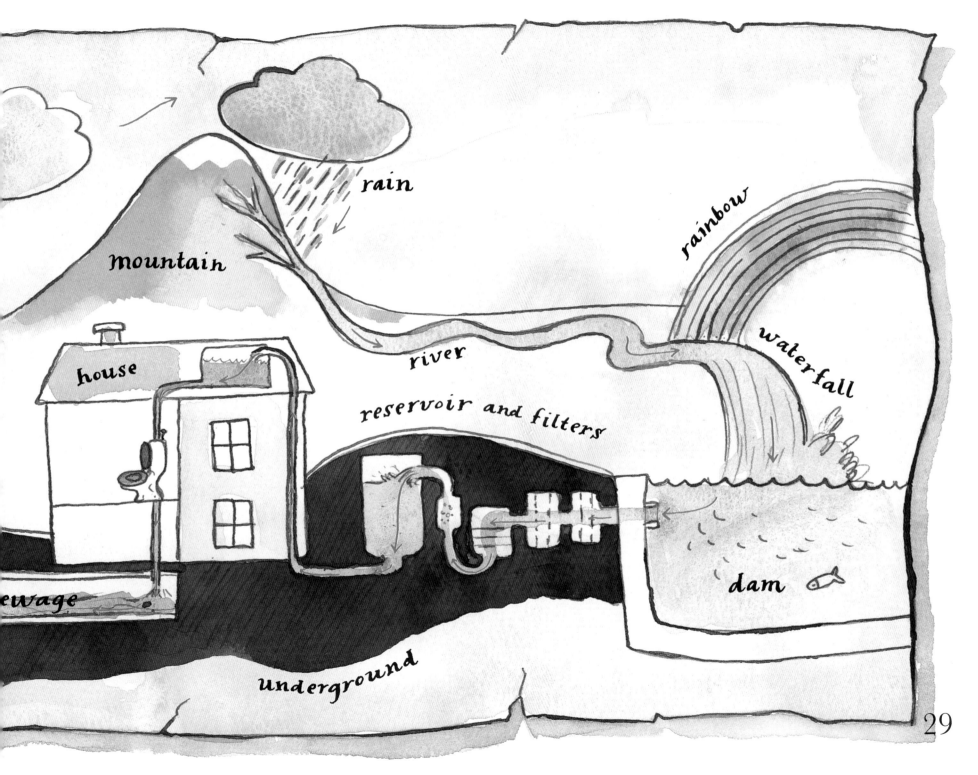

rain

mountain

rainbow

waterfall

river

house

reservoir and filters

sewage

dam

underground

29

Helpful words

Alligators are big animals like crocodiles (see page 23). They live in the United States of America or China.

Chlorine is a substance that is put into water to kill germs (see page 18).

Clouds are huge white or grey shapes made from millions of small drops of water (see pages 9-11).

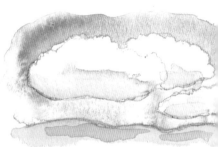

Coral reefs are made up of tiny sea animals that grow rocky shells and live together in warm seas (see page 7).

Dams and reservoirs are places where water is stored (see pages 14-17).

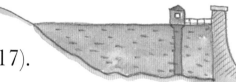

Evaporation is the way tiny drops of water are sucked into the air on warm days (see page 8). Tiny drops of water are also sucked out of plant leaves into the air on warm days (see page 28).

Ferries carry passengers and cars across stretches of water (see page 4).

Filter is a type of screen which keeps dirt back and lets clean water through (see pages 18, 25, 28)

Harbours and jetties are special sheltered places where boats are kept (see page 4).

Monsoons are rainstorms that last for months in some hot countries (see page 11).

Sewage is the dirty water from toilets and drains (see pages 22-25).

Sewage farm is where sewage water is cleaned (see pages 24-25).

Shipwreck is a sunken ship (see page 7).

Tugboats are used to tow other boats (see page 4).

Tanker ships carry oil and petrol across the sea (see page 4).

Tanker lorries carry liquids from place to place by road (see page 17).

U-bend is a pipe under the sink or a bath that keeps germs and smells from coming up the plughole (see page 20).

Water power the power of moving water can be used to turn a wheel or work a machine to make electricity (see pages 14-15).

For Albin and Gabriel

This edition 2014

First published by Franklin Watts,
338 Euston Road, London NW1 3BH

Franklin Watts Australia,
Level 17 / 207 Kent Street, Sydney NSW 2000

The illustrations in this book were made by Brita and Mick.
Find out more about Mick and Brita at www.mickandbrita.com

Series editor: Paula Borton
Art director: Robert Walster
Consultant: Peter Riley

A CIP catalogue record is available from the British Library.
Dewey Classification 553.7

Printed in China

ISBN 978 1 4451 2884 9

Franklin Watts is a division of Hachette Children's Books,
an Hachette UK company. www.hachette.co.uk